The Queen's Plan

Written by Alison Hawes

Illustrated by Clare Elsom

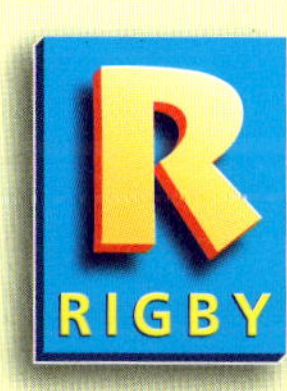

The queen cooks the food.

But she is not a good cook.

The king fixes things.

But he is no good with tools.

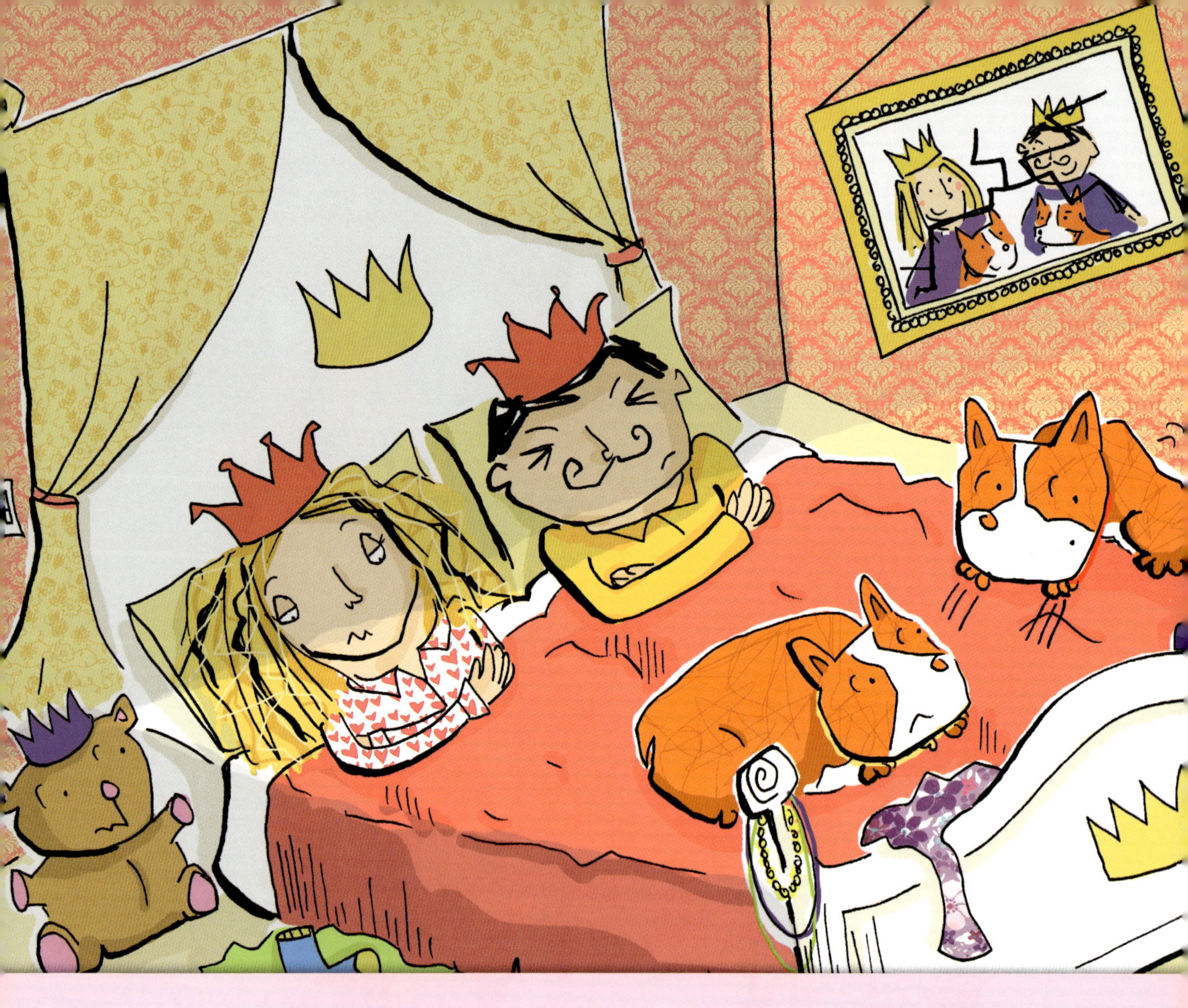

Soon, the queen and king
can not sleep.

They are in pain from the queen's cooking. They are fed up with the mess.

But the queen has a plan.
She sits upright and flicks on
the light.

We need to swop jobs!
I agree!

Soon, the queen is painting rooms ...

... and banging in nails.

Soon, the king is poaching eggs ...

... and roasting beef.

This food is good!

The queen and king agree
to keep to the plan.

Soon, they can sleep again at night.